GALE
CENGAGE Learning

M000205388

Novels for Students, Volume 5 Copyright Notice

Copyright © 1999

Gale Research
27500 Drake Rd.
Farmington Hills, MI 48331-3535

ISBN 0-7876-2115-3
ISSN 1094-3552

Printed in the United States of America.
1 0 9 8 7 6 5 4 3

The Outsiders

S. E. Hinton 1967

Introduction

S. E. Hinton irrevocably altered the course of juvenile literature in America with her first novel. *The Outsiders* was published when she was seventeen and was her stark answer to the fluffy high school stories about proms and dates typical of the 1960s. "Where is reality?" she asked in an essay explaining her motivation in the *New York Times Book Review.* In other narratives for teens, she could not find "the drive-in social jungle ... the behind-the-scenes politicking that goes on in big schools, the cruel social system," or the teenagers who lived in those settings. In contrast, her story was real, graphic, emotional, and true to the challenges of being a teenager in twentieth-century America. In addition, it was an exciting narrative that captured teenagers' attention. It drew a wide audience, particularly boys who were reluctant readers. Thirty years after its publication, the novel remains immensely popular and has sold more than four million copies in the United States. Its adaptation to film was a great success as well.

The novel is the story of a traumatic time in the life of a recently orphaned fourteen-year-old boy named Ponyboy Curtis. He lives on the East Side, a member of the lower class and a gang of "greasers." Quiet and dreamy, Ponyboy has conflicts with his older brother and guardian, Darrel, who keeps the family together. The greasers— whom Ponyboy distinguishes from "hoods"—are the heroes of the tale. Set against them are the upper-class socials, or Socs, who enjoy drinking, driving nice cars, and beating up greasers. The circumstances of this social situation result in the death of three teens. The story explores the themes of class conflict, affection, brotherly love, and coming of age in a way that young people readily appreciate. This novel's portrayal of disaffected youth has been criticized for its violent content, but it is now regarded as a classic of juvenile literature. It can be considered one of the first examples of the "young adult" genre, and after its publication literature for teens gained a new realism, depth, and respect for its audience.

Author Biography

Born in 1950, Susan Eloise Hinton was raised in Tulsa, Oklahoma. She was an avid reader as a child and experimented with writing by the time she turned ten. Her early stories were about cowboys and horses, and she preferred plots with rough riding and gunfights. When Hinton reached her teens, however, she could not find anything pleasing to read. Adult literature was still a bit too complicated for her, while literature for teens consisted of innocent tales about girls finding boyfriends. To please herself, she decided to create a different fictional universe from these annoying "Mary Jane goes to the prom" novels. She wanted to create a realistic story about being a teen. Additionally, like her character Ponyboy, she wanted to record some events of her high school years. She took inspiration from real events and people to create a story of class warfare between teens. After working on the novel for a year and a half and through four rewrites, she let a friend's mother read it. The mother liked it enough to refer her to an agent, Marilyn Marlow of the Curtis Brown Agency. A contract offering publication arrived during Hinton's high-school graduation ceremonies.

The Outsiders was published in 1967, when the author was just seventeen. Susan Eloise shortened her name to S. E. Hinton so that boys would not know the author was female. It was published to critical acclaim, won several awards, and became a cult classic among teen readers. The success of *The Outsiders* enabled Hinton to go to The University of Tulsa, where she earned a B.S. in Education in 1970. While in school she met her future husband, David Inhofe, who encouraged her to write her second novel, *That Was Then, This Is Now* (1971). Over the next decade, she published a new novel every four years. In 1975, she published *Rumble Fish*, and *Tex* in 1979. Although she was no longer an adolescent herself, Hinton was still able to bring her sympathy for teens and insight into their lives to her work. She only published one work in the 1980s, 1988's *Taming the Star Runner*, and in the 1990s she has focused more on picture books for younger readers than on novels.

Other than her writing, Hinton is kept busy by a family life and her son, Nicholas David. She has also served as a consultant on the film adaptations of her novels and has even appeared in minor roles. She continues to write and lives in Tulsa. Her pivotal role in the development of young adult fiction was recognized in 1988, when the American Library Association awarded her the first Margaret Edwards Young Adult Author Achievement Award for her body of work.

Plot Summary

The Greaser Gang

The Outsiders opens with the recollections of Ponyboy Curtis, the narrator of the story. He tells the reader in the first paragraph that he is a "greaser," from the poor neighborhood of his hometown. In the second paragraph, however, he explains that he is different from other greasers in his love of movies and books. Ponyboy is daydreaming after a Paul Newman movie when he is jumped by a gang of upper-class rich kids, known as socials, or "Socs." It is only the intervention of his two brothers and their friends that saves Ponyboy from being badly injured. The greasers have good reason to fear the Socs, a group of whom beat their friend Johnny so badly that he began to carry a switchblade wherever he went. Partly for this reason, Ponyboy's oldest brother Darry yells at him for going to the movies unaccompanied, and Pony relates that he feels that he can never please Darry.

On the next night, Pony and Johnny accompany Dallas Winston, the most hardened member of their gang, to a drive-in movie. There Dally begins to harass two Soc girls who are there without dates. After one of the girls, Cherry Valance, tells Dally to leave them alone, he leaves she and Ponyboy strike up a conversation. Dally returns, and when Johnny tells him to leave the girls alone, Dally stalks off for good. Later Two-Bit will join them, scaring Johnny in the process. Later Cherry asks, and Pony tells, why Johnny seems so jumpy and scared. After hearing how the Socs nearly killed Johnny, Cherry tells Ponyboy that "things are rough all over," but he does not believe her.

Greasers vs. Socs

After the movie, Cherry and Ponyboy share their thoughts on the differences between Greasers and Socs, and Ponyboy is surprised to find that they have similarities, too. The three greaser boys are walking Cherry and her friend Marcia to Two-Bit's car when they are spotted by the Socs. In order to avoid a fight, Cherry and Marcia agree to go home with the Socs and Two-Bit also goes home. Johnny and Ponyboy remain at the lot and talk about how things should be different before falling asleep. After Pony arrives home late, Darry confronts, then slaps him. Pony runs out of the house, and he and Johnny go to the park so Ponyboy can cool off before returning home.

In the park, Johnny and Ponyboy are accosted by drunken Socs. After they try to drown Ponyboy, Johnny kills one of them with his knife. The two decide to run away, and Dally helps them by telling them where to hide and giving them money and a gun. They hop a train to their hideout, a church in the country. There they cut and bleach their hair to disguise their identities. Pony feels that in losing his hair style, he has lost his identity, a feature that made him a greaser: "Our hair labeled us greasers, too— it was our trademark. Maybe we couldn't have Corvairs or madras shirts, but we could have hair."

Ponyboy and Johnny pass a lonely and bored four or five days at the church, reading to each other from *Gone with the Wind.* One morning the two boys watch a sunrise, which reminds Ponyboy of a Robert Frost poem, "Nothing Gold Can Stay," though he feels that the poem's deeper meaning escapes him. The next morning, Dally arrives and tells them that Cherry Valance will testify on their behalf. This prompts Johnny to say that they will turn themselves in. Dally tries to talk Johnny out of it, not wanting jail to harden him, but Johnny is determined. They are on their way back to the church when they realize that it is on fire and that a group of kids is trapped inside.

Hoods and Heroes

Ponyboy and Johnny manage to rescue all the kids in the church, but Pony faints after Johnny pushes him out the window. When he wakes up in ambulance, one of the teachers tells him that in spite of Dally's heroism in pulling Johnny from the flames, Johnny is in critical condition. Pony tells the disbelieving teacher that he and Johnny are wanted for murder. At the hospital, Pony is reunited with his brothers; when he sees Darry crying, he realizes the depth of Darry's love and concern for him.

Because of the publicity, Ponyboy realizes that he and his brothers could be separated. He also finds out that Sandy, Soda's girlfriend, has left town, and it is implied that she is pregnant. Later, Pony and Two-Bit encounter Randy, one of the Socs, who is tormented by his part in what has happened. He tells Pony that he could never have gone into the fire to rescue someone as Ponyboy and Johnny did. Two-Bit and Ponyboy then go to the hospital, and Pony realizes that Johnny is dying. Johnny's eyes glow when Pony tells him he's being called a hero, but when Johnny's mother comes to see him, he passes out from the strain of trying to refuse her visit. When Pony and Two-Bit then visit Dally in his room, Pony thinks of Dally as his buddy for the first time. Later, Two-Bit and Pony run into Cherry Valance, who assures them the score-settling rumble with the Socs won't involve weapons. She angers Pony when she says she won't visit Johnny in the hospital because he killed Bob. When Cherry weeps, Ponyboy tells her they both see the same sunset.

The rumble begins later that night when Darry squares off against an old friend of his from high school. Dally runs up to join the rumble and helps Pony fight one of the Socs. He then takes Pony to see Johnny at the hospital to tell him of their victory. Johnny tells them that fighting does no good and then instructs Ponyboy to "stay gold" before he dies. The one thing he loves gone, Dally runs out of the room in agony. After Ponyboy arrives home, the gang gets a call from Dally, who has just robbed a store. They arrive at the vacant lot in time to see Dally killed in a shootout with the police, and Pony faints at the scene of Dally's death.

"Staying Gold"

Ponyboy is still recovering when he is visited by Randy, who leaves when he realizes that Ponyboy is trying to deny that Johnny is dead. Pony plans to confess to killing Bob at the hearing inquiring into the incident, but he is not questioned about it. Pony and his brothers are granted permission to remain together, but Pony continues to have trouble recovering. He tries to write an essay so he can pass English, but finds all the possible topics either meaningless or too painful. After Pony and Darry argue again, Soda uncharacteristically explodes in anger, and Ponyboy learns that Sandy was cheating on Soda. She will not answer Soda's letters, and the baby she is carrying is not his. Ponyboy has been oblivious to Soda's pain, and after Soda tells them that without each other, they'll end up like Dally, they vow to fight less often.

Shortly after the family reconciliation, Ponyboy picks up Johnny's copy of *Gone with the Wind.* Inside, he finds a letter from Johnny, in which he tells Pony to let Dally know that it was worth it to rescue the children from the church, and that Pony can be whatever he wants to be in life, even though he is a greaser. Ponyboy finally realizes what it means to "stay gold." He begins to write his English theme, thinking of all the kids who need to know there is good in the world. He begins with the day that he walked out of the Paul Newman movie, forever changed by all that has happened since.

Characters

Randy Adderson

Randy is Bob's best friend and takes his death very hard. Before the rumble, he has a talk with Ponyboy about all that has happened. He has decided that violence is wrong because "it doesn't do any good." He stays out of the rumble and later comes to visit Pony when he's sick. His words lead Pony to realize that "the other guy was human too."

Johnny Cade

Beaten by his father and ignored by his mother, he stays around town only because he is the gang's pet, "everyone's kid brother." Johnny reminds Pony of a "little dark puppy that has been kicked too many times and is lost in a crowd of strangers." He was jumped once by the Socs and beaten very badly. Since then he has carried a blade and has become even more suspicious and jumpy. Johnny and Pony are friends by default. They are the youngest in the gang and also the most sensitive. They are quiet around the older boys and reflective between themselves.

Johnny echoes Pony's frustration at their predicament in life, scared of being beaten or killed and not able to change anything about it. Johnny was considered dumb by his teachers, and yet he realizes things that completely pass by Pony. While Pony reads from *Gone with the Wind* about Southern gentlemen riding into certain death, Johnny sees Dally. And when Pony recites Robert Frost, Johnny understands the meaning of the poem. They have to stay gold, stay young, and stay true to themselves. It is this message that Johnny sends to Pony in his final letter and the one Pony is left to struggle with.

Darrel Curtis

Darry has been taking care of the family ever since Mr. and Mrs. Curtis died in a car wreck, eight months before the start of the novel. A judge allows the brothers to stay together under twenty-year-old Darry's supervision—so long as they stay out of trouble. Rather than go to college on a football scholarship, Darry has to go to work in order to keep the three together and Pony in school. He has had to give up a lot and has become an adult too fast. "Darry's hard and firm and rarely grins at all." A big and powerful young man, Darry has "eyes that are like two pieces of pale blue-green ice.... He doesn't understand anything that is not plain hard fact. But he uses his head." Darry takes his custodianship very seriously by keeping a tight hold on Pony.

Ponyboy often has conflicts with his oldest brother, not realizing how similar the two are. Darry is different from the other greasers; as Two-Bit says, "the only thing that keeps Darry from being a

Soc is us." He is the leader of the gang by mutual consent and respect. He wears his hair short like a Soc and he is clean shaven. While Darry likes fighting for the athletic challenge of it, Pony realizes that Darry is too smart to stay around the greasers forever. "That's why he's better than the rest of us, [Pony] thought. He's going somewhere." Pony finally comes to understand his brother really does love him.

Darry Curtis

See Darrel Curtis

Ponyboy Curtis

The story is Ponyboy Curtis's narrative about his experience seeing three young men die. Pony is a good student, a track star, and a greaser. It is this latter distinction, rather than his orphan status, which brings him trouble. In addition, he is a solitary, sensitive boy who likes movies, watching sunsets, and reading. His consumption of these poetic pursuits often foils his common sense. Thus, his desire to see movies without the distracting fidgets of friends or brothers leads to his lonely walk home from the cinema and his run in with a group of Socs. Luckily for him, his brothers and the gang hear his cries for help and he doesn't receive anything like the beating that spooked Johnny.

A great deal of the tension in Pony comes from his attempts to figure out his oldest brother Darry.

He complains to Two-Bit, Johnny, and Cherry that his brother doesn't like him. He believes that Darry resents him because he had to turn down a football scholarship to college in order to support him. Everyone tries to tell him otherwise, but Pony doesn't believe in Darry's love for him until he is injured in the fire. Even so, he only comes to understand his brother after their fighting drives Sodapop, the middle brother, to tears.

The beauty of Ponyboy's character is that though he emerges strong and confident at the end of the book, it is not the result of becoming a tough hood but of remaining true to himself. The positive tone is not so much because the Socs are beaten (this time), or that the boys will remain together, or that Ponyboy recovers from his injuries. Instead, the resolution is excruciatingly personal. When he scares off a bunch of Socs with a broken bottle, he considers his act no big deal: "anyone else could have done the same thing." This scares Two-Bit, because none of the gang wants Pony to become just another greaser. However, Two-Bit relaxes when he sees Pony stoop down and clean up the glass shards so that no one will get hurt. Ponyboy has, as Johnny would say, stayed golden. The real denouement of Pony's character growth is the resolution of tension between him and Darry. It tries to come once, when he hugs him at the hospital, but does not arrive until they chase down Soda. The three have a heart-to-heart talk and when Darry says "Sure, little buddy," thus calling Pony by the name reserved for Soda, Pony knows everything will be okay. "I reckon we all just wanted to stay together."

Sodapop Curtis

Ponyboy's older brother is sixteen going on seventeen and a high school dropout. He is the caregiver and peacemaker of the Curtis brothers. Soda is "movie-star kind of handsome, the kind that people stop on the street to watch go by." Bubbly like his name, Soda is "always happy-go-lucky and grinning" and the type of person who doesn't drink alcohol because "he gets drunk on just plain living." He listens to everyone, "understands everybody," and is Pony's confidante. Soda enjoys teasing Darry and is the only one who would dare do so. He also gives Darry backrubs after he has tried to carry too much roofing material at work. However, being caught between Darry and Pony is draining. He also has to suffer in silence when his girlfriend, Sandy, is shipped to Florida.

Media Adaptations

- *The Outsiders* was made into a film starring C. Thomas Howell, Matt Dillon, Ralph Macchio, Patrick Swayze, Rob Lowe, Diane Lane, Tom Cruise, and Emilio Estevez. The 1983 Warner Brothers film, directed by Francis Ford Coppola, was a huge success and remains a popular film.

- Fox-TV adapted the novel as a television series in 1990.

- *The Outsiders* was also made into a filmstrip with cassette in 1978 by Current Affairs/Mark Twain Media, and as an audiocassette for Random House, 1993.

Paul Holden

In the big confrontation between Socs and greasers after Bob Sheldon's death, Darry is put forth as the rumble starter. Paul steps up to answer for the Socs. While in high school, the two were friends and teammates on the football team. Now Paul shows hatred, contempt, and pity for his old friend.

Johnnycakes

See Johnny Cade

Marcia

She is a friend of Cherry's who seems like a good match for Two-Bit when they meet at the drive-in. However, social reality will keep them from getting together.

Two-Bit Matthews

See Keith Matthews

Keith Matthews

The funny guy of the gang who always has to make his "two bits" worth of smart remarks. His specialty is shoplifting, which he does for the challenge of it. He likes "fights, blondes, and for some unfathomable reason, school."

Buck Merrill

Dally's Rodeo partner is the source of the cash Johnny and Pony use to hide out after the killing of Bob Sheldon.

Steve Randle

Soda's best friend and another greaser, Steve works part-time at the gas station where Soda works full-time. His specialty is cars. Between Soda's looks and Steve's mechanical aptitude, their station is the most popular in town. Ponyboy only likes Steve because of Soda; Steve treats Pony like a tagalong when Soda brings him on their escapades.

Sandy

Soda's girlfriend who, later in the novel, leaves for Florida. It is implied that she is pregnant, and Soda has offered to marry her. But she returns his letters unopened and Soda discovers someone else is most likely the father.

Bob Sheldon

The rich, handsome, and arrogant Soc who is responsible for the serious damage done to Johnny one night. Bob is also Cherry's boyfriend; although she doesn't want to see him when he has been drinking, she says otherwise he is sweet and friendly. He has a set of rings he wears to make his hitting all the more damaging. Johnny kills Bob to save Pony.

Curly Shepard

Tim's younger brother, "an average downtown hood, tough and not very bright." He and Pony have a mutual respect for each other after they once burned each other on a dare. Like Darry does for Pony, Curly's older brother Tim keeps an eye out for his sibling. While Pony and Curly are in similar positions—they are being brought up and protected by powerful older brothers—Curly is always in and out of the reformatory.

Tim Shepard

The leader of another gang of Greasers who ally themselves with Darry's gang. He "looked like the model JD you see in films and magazines" and is "one of those who enjoy being a hood." Tim demands the discipline and code one normally imagines a gang to have. That is, his gang is not a loose group of childhood friends like Darry's. He has broken a few of Dally's ribs in one of the regular fights they have just for fun. Nevertheless, he and Dally are good friends. When the rumble is scheduled, it is Tim who brings in his troops and another gang to bring the greaser total to twenty.

Mr. Syme

Ponyboy's English teacher, whose assignment leads to the narrative of the novel. He is concerned about Pony's slumping grades, and "you can tell he's interested in you as a person, too."

Cherry Valance

See Sherri Valance

Sherri Valance

Cherry is a pretty, red-headed Soc whom Pony and Johnny meet at the drive-in. Although she responds negatively to Dally's crude come-ons, she tells Pony that she could easily fall in love with him. Cherry hates fighting and serves as a go-between for the two groups. She doesn't succeed in stopping the fighting, but she does help increase understanding. She delivers two important revelations to Pony. The first is that Socs are not without their own problems, and the other is that rich people are capable of watching sunsets, just as Pony does.

Dally Winston

See Dallas Winston

Dallas Winston

"The real character of the gang," Dally was arrested his first time at the age of ten. He spent three years on the "wild side" of New York and likes to blow off steam in gang fights. He is the most dangerous member of the bunch—not even Darry wants to tangle with him—but he is still a part of their greaser "family." The local police have a large file on him, and he has just gotten out of jail at the opening of the novel. While "the fight for self-preservation had hardened him beyond caring," there are two things that have meaning for him: jockeying on ponies (the "only thing Dally did honestly") and Johnny.

In Tulsa, lacking a rival gang, Dally hates the Socs. Fighting them is frustrating, however, because he knows that beating them doesn't take away any of their social advantages. During fights he takes particular care to look out for Johnny, and so he helps the boys after the murder even though it could return him to prison. Johnny returns Dally's care with a devoted admiration. Consequently, Johnny views him as a heroic gentleman of courage, like those in *Gone with the Wind.* When Johnny is dead the rest of the gang realizes he was Dally's breaking point. Having lost the one thing he really cared about, Dally sets himself up for death. After robbing a store, he threatens the pursuing cops with an empty gun. He dies in front of his friends in a hail of bullets.

Jerry Wood

One of the few adults in the novel, Jerry Wood is a teacher at the scene of the fire. He stays by Pony in the ambulance and the hospital and listens to his tale.

Class Conflict

Issues of American economic class are confronted head on by the portrayal of the rival gangs as rich and poor. The rich Socs "jump greasers and wreck houses and throw beer blasts for kicks, and get editorials in the paper for being a public disgrace one day and an asset to society the next." The poor greasers, conversely, "steal things and drive old souped-up cars and hold up gas stations and have a gang fight once in a while." Each group views the other as the enemy and "that's just the way things are." But circumstances will at least reveal to a few that everyone is human—although there will still be a rivalry.

Cherry offers her opinion that it is not just a difference in money: "You greasers have a different set of values. You're more emotional. We're sophisticated—cool to the point of not feeling anything.... Rat race is a perfect name for [our life]." This leads Pony to wonder if perhaps it is just natural for the two classes to be separate and unequal—a fact that haunts Johnny's decision to turn himself in. He knows that the courts stereotype all greasers as juvenile delinquents. Still, Ponyboy comes to understand that Socs and Greasers have similarities: "It seemed funny to me that the sunset she saw from her patio and the one I saw from the back steps was the same one. Maybe the two different worlds we lived in weren't so different. We saw the same sunset."

Topics for Further Study

- Reflect on the significance of the title—who are the outsiders, and what are they outside of? What does it mean to be an outsider and why has this become a twentieth-century phenomenon? Support your arguments with examples from recent history.

- There are two famous novels with similar titles to Hinton's story. Both concern young men, circumstantial murder(s), and existentialism (the philosophy that the individual is solely responsible for his fate). The two novels are Richard Wright's *The*

Outsider and Albert Camus's *The Stranger* (published in England as *The Outsider)*. Compare Hinton's novel with one of these other "outsider" stories.

- Many people deny that social or economic class plays a significant role in American society or government. Using examples from this novel and other teenage books or films (such as *The Breakfast Club* and *Pretty In Pink* through the recent *Clueless)*, argue whether you think this is true or false.

- Compare and contrast *The Outsiders* with another story of gangs, such as *Boys in the Hood* or *West Side Story.* Compare specific events, characters, and themes.

- Juvenile crime and "youth predators" have become an obsessive political issue over the last decade. Are youth today really more violent than twenty or thirty years ago? Do some research into the phenomenon of youth violence and some of the following topics: trying youths as young as twelve as adults; incarcerating teens with adults; and increasing security at school versus increasing education spending increases. Good sources to start with are the National Center for Juvenile Justice (http://www.ncjj.org) and the Center on Juvenile Justice and Criminal Justice (http://www.cjcj.org).

That is as far as the bridge is going to extend between the two worlds. Cherry warns that in public she will have to appear to ignore him as usual, "it's not personal or anything." Pony then says Two-bit is smart for throwing away a false phone number Marcia gave him: "he knew the score." To give her credit, Cherry does act as a go-between in terms of the rumble, but there is no hint of change. Indeed, Cherry's help may simply be an attempt to appease her own conscience. Finally, all contact is lost after Bob's death. Cherry cannot bear to resume the effort of bridging the gap with the group who killed her boyfriend—despite the fact that Bob brought it on himself.

In sum, the portrayal of class that Hinton makes simply outlines the facts. There is no attempt to suggest a way of bringing the classes together. Nor is there a criticism of either side, because both sides are at fault. The only optimism this novel offers is that members of the two sides can learn to understand one another, even if they still fight. In the end, greasers will be greasers and Socs will be Socs.

Search for Self

Ponyboy has all the worries of a boy his age; is he strong, brave, or handsome enough to match up to the masculine ideal? In Pony's case, the ideal is a cross between Soda and Darry. He wants to be handsome and appealing to everyone but he also wants to be tough, full of sense, and a good fighter. He is none of these things. Everyone in the gang is cautious around Pony because they already recognize that he is something special in his own right. As Two-bit says, in response to a headline, "Y'all were heroes from the beginning." Pony doesn't seem to understand this, however. When others tell him they are impressed by his rescue of the children, Pony shrugs and says that anyone would have done the same. But not everyone would have rushed into a flaming building to rescue someone they didn't know; few also have the courage, to hold off a gang of Socs. The brilliance of this last episode is how it reveals Pony is learning something which he sensed at the rumble, but only confronts in the writing of the tale.

In this last confrontation, Pony makes the Socs back down with a broken bottle, giving every appearance of having become a young tough hood. Two-Bit witnesses this and is concerned: "Ponyboy, listen, don't get tough. You're not like the rest of us and don't try to be...." But tough hoods don't get hurt, Pony thinks in response. They also do not pick up glass shards off the street, which Pony proceeds to do. This relieves Two-Bit, who suddenly realizes Pony is still himself, although he won't take anymore trouble from the Socs. In other words, he can act tough enough to survive, but it is just an act

—Pony is still the one who remains considerate, stays gold, reads poetry, and picks up the glass. "I didn't want anyone to get a flat tire."

Loyalty

The tenderness with which the gang regards its respective members is endearing. They are all tough guys, but they all really care about each other. It is a gang community of greasers that wants, subtly, to change their group. They will do it through the youngest and brightest members, Johnny and Pony. Darry wants his younger brother to amount to something and Dally wants Johnny to have a better life. "I just don't want you to get hurt," Dally says when Johnny speaks of turning himself in. "You get hardened in jail. I don't want that to happen to you."

In some ways, then, the group understands the cycle of violence and wants it to stop. Unfortunately, they do not have the family, financial, or community support to make changes, and they realize that they must be satisfied with each other. By this standard the novel ends happily. It is this communal love that enables Johnny to survive a rough home life and die peacefully. "Dally was proud of him. That was all Johnny had ever wanted." Dally's loss of the one person he cares about drives him to a fatal confrontation with police. It is this same community recognition that Pony seeks, and finally gets, from Darry. The brothers realize that "if we don't have each other, we don't have anything." There is some hope that together they will be okay.

Style

Narration

Ponyboy narrates the story in retrospect, under the guise of having to write out a theme for English class. This presentation of a story by one of the characters involved is called first-person narrative. A first-person narrative is easily identified by the use of "I" in telling the story. Having one of the characters tell the story can make the story more immediate for readers, because they easily can put themselves in the narrator's place.

A first-person narrator also means a limited perspective, however. Ponyboy can only describe his own thoughts and can only relate events he has witnessed or heard about. This limited perspective lends itself very well to the themes of class conflict that appear throughout the book. At the beginning of the story, Pony can only sympathize with other greasers. A third-person narrator ("he/she said") who knows about all of the characters could tell the reader what Cherry or Randy or even Sodapop was thinking. Instead, Pony has to learn to understand other people's feelings all by himself. This understanding is an important part of his coming of age.

Characters

Hinton is a character writer instead of an idea writer. She develops her characters in depth and then lets them create the story. Consequently, the opening of the book is a very detailed introduction to each character. By the end of the book, the reader knows each character in intimate detail. In addition, the characters' names are particularly descriptive. "Ponyboy," for instance, creates an image of a youth becoming a cowboy. Sodapop's name reflects his own bubbly personality. Even "Dallas Winston," the combination of a Texas city and a famous cigarette brand, invokes bygone days of Western heroics and toughness. This invocation ties in with Hinton's fascination with that earlier rough and violent era.

Description and Diction

The brief detail used in the book is rather startling in its effectiveness. Just as Ponyboy can "get [Dally's] personality down in a few lines" of a drawing, he can sum up his friends in just a few words. Johnny, for instance, is "a little dark puppy that has been kicked too many times and is lost in a crowd of strangers." The speed of slang adjectives adds another dimension to description. "Greasers. You know, like hoods, JD's," for example, gives Mr. Wood a short but precise description of the boys' background.

The scene of heroic rescue is full of delightful phrasing. The comparison of the burning church to hell might be expected, but the simile of falling cinders as biting ants is rather novel. Adding realism to tension occurs in a truism: "I picked up a kid, and he promptly bit me." And a reaction to Two-Bit's drinking, "I'd hate to see the day when I had to get my nerve from a can," sounds like a wise saying. Hinton is successful in using youth slang in her prose style and this success makes the narrative more believable.

Allusions

Allusions are references to other works of literature or art. A narrator can use them to explain a character or situation by comparing it to something already known by the reader. Ponyboy refers to several other works of literature to make comparisons as well as to avoid lengthy explanations. For instance, he refers to Charles Dickens's novel *Great Expectations*, another tale of class conflict: "That kid Pip, he reminded me of us —the way he felt marked lousy because he wasn't a gentleman or anything, and the way that girl kept looking down on him." While Johnny and Ponyboy are hiding out at the church, they discuss two works: the novel *Gone with the Wind* and the poem "Nothing Gold Can Stay." Johnny sees echoes of the Southern gentlemen's gallantry in Dally's coolness, and the sunrise reminds Ponyboy of the poem. It is only later, with Johnny's help, that Pony comes to understand the meaning of the poem. In this way, an allusion has helped illustrate the coming of age theme of the novel.

Imagery

Imagery is using visual images, sometimes called symbols, to reinforce themes or represent deeper meanings. The novel does not contain many symbols, because the story is simply a recounting of what happened. There is one overriding image in the story, however, one which is important to the main characters and the main theme. The image is that of a sunrise or sunset. Once again, the myth of the cowboy is suggested. Our heroes should ride off safely into the sunset, just like the heroes of Western movies. Unfortunately, not all of the gang will make that ride. Sunsets also figure in the novel because Pony likes to watch them. This signifies that he is a sensitive boy who appreciates beauty. But he is not alone in his appreciation. He discovers that a Soc, Cherry, is capable of watching a sunset. Given the chance, so is Johnny. The sunrise that Johnny and Pony share at the church prompts recitation of a Robert Frost poem, "Nothing Gold can Stay." That poem sums up the meaning of the sunset in this story and is the theme Pony is trying to develop for his English teacher. For Johnny and Pony, the phrase comes to mean that good things don't last. Sunsets are short, and blissful escapes into abandoned churches end in fire. But it is possible, Pony proves, to remain true to one's self and thereby "stay gold."

The Rise of Youth Culture

In the United States, the period from 1945 to 1963 was termed the "Baby Boom" because of the sharp increase in the number of children born during those years. By 1958, one-third of the country's population was fifteen years old or younger. The years after World War II had also seen an increase in wealth throughout the United States. By the time they became teenagers in the late 1950s and early 1960s, therefore, many of these "Baby Boomers" had plenty of spare cash to spend. Companies competed to attract the dollars of these new consumers. The film, music, television, and fashion industries created products especially for the increasingly influential teen market. Rock 'n' roll became the most popular music on the radio, and movies also reflected this new focus on adolescents. Actors James Dean and Marlon Brando became idols for portraying teenage antiheroes in *Rebel without a Cause* (1955) and *The Wild One* (1954). Paul Newman, whose looks Ponyboy admires as "tough," followed in the footsteps of these actors by playing similarly cool characters in the films *The Hustler* (1961), *Hud* (1963), and *Cool Hand Luke* (1967).

Teenagers' increased spending power also gave them a new measure of independence from their parents. Rebellion against adult authority became a notable theme in many teen films. Loud rock 'n' roll music became another way for teens to defy their parents' values. Some adolescents' rebellion turned violent, and teenage gangs sprouted in urban areas. The increase in the numbers of young people meant an increase in juvenile delinquents as well. These "JDs" became an urgent concern for law enforcement in the 1950s and 1960s. As *The Outsiders* demonstrates, however, not all of these delinquents were from poor neighborhoods. Children from supposedly "good families" also became dropouts, gang members, and drug or alcohol abusers.

The Vietnam War and the Protest Movement

Teenagers were not the only Americans who challenged authority in the 1960s. The public in general had begun to question U.S. involvement in Vietnam's war against communist rebels. The United States had been providing military advisors to this southeast Asian country since the 1950s. In 1964, however, the number of U.S. troops in Vietnam doubled. By 1967, almost half a million Americans were fighting in Vietnam. Nevertheless, many citizens had doubts as to the effectiveness and morality of American involvement. Protesters turned up in the thousands for antiwar demonstrations. The protesters came from all walks of life: groups included those made up of students, clergy, scientists, and women.

The year 1967 featured many notable protests. University of Wisconsin students destroyed university property while running recruiters from Dow Chemical (the makers of the defoliant napalm) off campus. The week of April 15 saw antiwar demonstrations in New York and San Francisco bring out 100,000 and 20,000 people respectively. A protest at the Pentagon led to arrests of several notable people, including poet Allen Ginsberg and pediatrician Dr. Benjamin Spock. The Reverend Martin Luther King, Jr., proposed a merging of the civil rights movement and the antiwar movement. He declared the U.S. government "the greatest purveyor of violence in the world."

Compare & Contrast

- **1967:** Romanticized movies of teen rebellion give way to upbeat musicals extolling a life of beach parties, fast cars, and teen relationships.
  1990s: One of the most popular genres for teens is the horror movie, in which a group of teens is pitted against a homicidal maniac. The 1996 film *Scream* becomes one of the top grossing releases of the year, earning over $100 million in box office receipts.

- **1967:** The Beatles lead the "British

Invasion" of American music as they dominate the pop charts. Their 1967 album *Sgt. Pepper's Lonely Hearts Club Band* uses several experimental recording techniques and influences countless pop and rock artists.

1990s: Popular music has broken down into countless genres, with no one type dominating the market. Rap, "alternative," rhythm and blues, pop, rock, and movie soundtrack albums all reach number one at various times during the decade.

- **1967:** Dropout rates show a sharp increase, and by the late 1960s over 7.5 million students have left high school before graduating. In 1967, 15 percent of white students are dropouts, as opposed to almost 30 percent of black students (Hispanic rates were not recorded at this time). **1990s:** In 1996, the overall dropout rate remains steady at five percent, or about 500,000 students yearly. Dropout rates for both black and white students have decreased, to 6.7 and 4.1 percent respectively; the Hispanic dropout rate remains higher, at 9 percent. Low income students have the highest dropout rate of any group: 11.1 percent.

- **1967:** In an America torn by

political protest, race riots, and growing recreational drug use, teenage gangs seem a minor menace in comparison. Schools are relatively safe, as violent confrontations most often occur between gangs outside of school property.

1990s: Teenage gang violence is an increasing problem for both urban and rural communities. Gang violence often erupts inside schools and sometimes involves innocent bystanders. Easy access to drugs and guns leads to deaths inside school buildings and on school grounds.

- **1967:** The People's Republic of China explodes its first hydrogen bomb, raising U.S. concerns and Soviet fears of another contender in the nuclear arms race.

  1990s: A clear sign that nonproliferation treaties have failed to stop the spread of nuclear weapons, in 1998 first India and then Pakistan conduct nuclear tests and declare themselves nuclear states.

Race Relations in the 1960s

Although all of the "greaser" characters in *The Outsiders* are white, the prejudice they endure recalls that suffered by African Americans and other nonwhites during the same era. Several laws and court decisions of the late 1950s and early 1960s had outlawed public segregation. Nevertheless, discrimination was still part of daily life for many blacks in the 1960s. In some southern cities, public school integration had to be enforced by federal troops. Black students who attended previously allwhite schools often faced ridicule and even physical abuse from their classmates. (This calls to mind how Ponyboy is called a "hood" by his lab partner when he uses a switchblade to dissect a worm in biology class.)

Despite the political gains made by the civil rights movement, practical gains for African Americans lagged far behind. According to census statistics of the 1960s, almost one-half of nonwhite households were below the poverty line, compared to one-fifth of white households. Unemployment rates among nonwhites were more than double that of whites, at 7.3 percent. "White flight" occurred as white middle-class families moved from the city to the suburbs. As a result, many companies and stores moved out of the cities as well, leading to a decline in investment in infrastructure. The poor families left behind, both black and white, often ended up with poorer schools, fewer government resources, and decaying neighborhoods. Thus, while political segregation was outlawed, economic segregation was still in place.

Race riots sometimes erupted in these impoverished neighborhoods, often provoked by incidents of police brutality. The most devastating of these incidents was the Watts riot that took place over six days in 1965. The Los Angeles police required the assistance of the California National Guard to halt this disturbance, which left thirtyfour dead, thousands injured, and over forty million dollars of property damage. In 1967, race riots erupted in several U.S. cities, leaving eighty-three dead and several hundred injured. These riots were different from the "rumbles" portrayed in *The Outsiders*, which are essentially conflicts between rival gangs. These race riots of the 1960s, on the other hand, usually began as conflicts between white police and black residents. As the conflict grew, rioters targeted innocent bystanders and property as well. Shops were looted and burned, even those owned by black families living in the neighborhoods. One result of these riots was the Anti-Riot Act, which was added to the Civil Rights Bill of 1968.

Critical Overview

Although *The Outsiders* has been a favorite with teens ever since its publication in 1967, adult critics have been more cautious in their assessments. Initial reviews debated the supposed "realism" of this startling new work, as well as the skill of its young author. Thomas Fleming, for instance, questioned Hinton's portrayal of the Soc-Greaser conflict. He noted that in his hometown it was the poor kids who beat up the rich ones, not the other way around. Nevertheless, he added in his *New York Times Book Review* assessment that "Hinton' s fire-engine pace does not give the reader much time to manufacture doubts." Nat Hentoff similarly observed in *Atlantic Monthly* that the plot of the book was "factitious," or forced and artificial. He praised the author, however, for addressing issues of class that were absent in previous books for teens: "Any teenager, no matter what some of his textbooks say, knows that this is decidedly not a classless society." *School Library Journal* contributor Lillian Gerhardt similarly hailed Hinton's portrayal of class rivalry: "It is rare-to-unique among juvenile books ... to find a novel confronting class hostilities which have intensified since the Depression."

In another early review, William Jay Jacobs favorably compared *The Outsiders* with a popular classic from the 1950s, J. D. Salinger's *Catcher in the Rye*. Other critics have observed similarities between Hinton's Ponyboy and Salinger's Holden Caufield. "But as much as the sensitive, thoughtful Ponyboy resembles Holden, his [environment] is irrevocably different," Jacobs noted in *Teachers College Record.* "All around him are hostility and fear, along with distrust for the 'system'." The critic did fault some of the dialogue as "false" and the themes as a bit too "profound" for "hoods." Nevertheless, he noted that the novel had a more mature tone than most first novels, and had "relevance for today's [society]."

By 1970, *The Outsiders* had already been identified as a powerful influence on young adult literature. Many critics questioned whether it and other examples of the "New Realism" were a positive influence on teens. Attempts to ban the book were made in various places. As a result, many reviews of the time were particularly negative. For instance, a *Times Literary Supplement* critic worried that young readers "will waive literary discriminations about a book of this kind and adopt Ponyboy as a kind of folk hero for both his exploits and his dialogue." Other critics faulted the slang dialogue and sometimes moralizing tone. In his *Children's Book News* review, Aidan Chambers noted that the book was flawed because it was written with self-indulgence "and could profitably have been cut." Nevertheless, reviewers could not deny the appeal the book had for teen readers. As Chambers added, the first-person narrative had "interesting qualities," such as compassion and lots of action.

Critics have also recognized, however, that the strength of *The Outsiders* lies in its characters. In her 1969 work *Children's Reading in the Home*, May Hill Arbuthnot praises the book's "incisive portraits of individual boys growing up in a hostile environment.... The characters are unforgettable." Alethea K. Helbig and Agnes Regan Perkins made a similar observation in their 1986 work *Dictionary of American Children's Fiction.* They remarked that while some of the incidents in the plot seem unbelievable, "they hold up well during reading, probably because the author makes Pony's concerns and the warm relationship between the brothers seem very real." Cynthia Rose likewise stated in *Monthly Film Bulletin* that Hinton's "characterisation of the emotional claustrophobia and relentlessly limited prospects of the poor white world— where sacrifice so often defines love—is her most impressive literary achievement."

Hinton's novel has maintained its popularity for over thirty years, leading later critics to analyze its appeal. In a 1986 *Nation* article, Michael Malone suggested that it was because *The Outsiders* conforms to the popular myth of "the tragic beauty of violent youth." He observed that rather than being realistic, Ponyboy's language and story belong to a mythic or ideal world where teens anguish over their problems without adults to hinder or help them. Nevertheless, Malone added that Hinton's ability "to evoke for her audience how teenagers feel about those clashes [of ideals] is indisputable." On the other hand, critic Michele Landsberg called Ponyboy's many poetic descriptions, particularly those of the greasers' appearance, "simply absurd." She explained in her *Reading for the Love of It* that Hinton's book "flatters the egos of young male readers with its barely-subliminal sexual praise, and lets them escape into the fantasized glory of attention and approval from an older teenage tough."

Other critics have found true literary merit in the novel, however, merit that explains its longlasting popularity. As Jay Daly observed in his *Presenting S. E. Hinton:* "It has nothing to do with the age of the author, and little to do with the so-called 'realism' of the setting. It does, however, have very much to do with the characters she creates, their humanity, and it has everything to do with her honesty." "One of Susan Hinton's significant achievements in *The Outsiders* is to hold up for scrutiny young people from economically, culturally, and socially deprived circumstances," John S. Simmons claimed in *Censored Books: Critical Viewpoints.* "In Ponyboy Curtis, his brothers Sodapop and Darry, and his 'Greaser' companions, Hinton has introduced readers, most of whom have probably been from white, middle class origins, to the desires, the priorities, the frustrations, the preoccupations, and above all, the *anger* of those young people who may live in the seedier parts of town but who have established a code of behavior which reflects (to the dismay of some) their sense of dignity and self-worth.... Most important, they believe in, trust, and support each other, all sentiments which can be universally admired despite the circumstances in which they are displayed."

Hinton herself has always known the key to her success. "Teenagers should not be written down to," she wrote in the *New York Times Book Review* upon the publication of *The Outsiders.* As a result, Hinton is an amazingly popular writer amongst teens and, especially, reluctant readers. Librarians and teachers use her books frequently for reading assignments. Hinton sums up the attraction to her action packed gang thrillers, saying: "Anyone can tell when [a teen's] intelligence is being underestimated. Those who are not ready for adult novels can easily have their love of reading killed by the inane junk lining the teenage shelf in the library." So she has gained the devotion of teen readers by following her own advice: "Earn respect by giving it."

Sources

May Hill Arbuthnot, in her *Children's Reading in the Home*, Scott, Foresman, 1969, pp. 174–75.

Aidan Chambers, review of *The Outsiders, Children's Book News*, Vol. 5, No. 6, November-December, 1970, p. 280.

Jay Daly, in his *Presenting S. E. Hinton*, Twayne Publishers, 1987.

Thomas Fleming, a review of *The Outsiders*, in the *New York Times Book Review*, Part II, May 7, 1967, pp. 10, 12.

Lillian V. Gerhardt, a review of *The Outsiders*, in the *School Library Journal*, Vol. 13, No. 9, May, 1967, pp. 64–65.

Alethea K. Helbig and Agnes Regan Perkins, 'The Outsiders," in their *Dictionary of American Children's Fiction, 1960-1984: Recent Books of Recognized Merit*, Greenwood Press, 1986, pp. 495–96.

Nat Hentoff, a review of *The Outsiders*, in the *Atlantic Monthly*, December, 1967, pp. 401–402.

Susan Eloise Hinton, "Teen Agers Are for Real," *New York Times Book Review*, August, 1967, pp. 26–29.

William Jay Jacobs, "Reading the Unreached," *Teachers College Record*, Vol. 69, No. 2, November, 1967, pp. 201–202.

Michele Landsberg, "Growing Up," in her *Reading for the Love of It: Best Books for Young Readers*, Prentice Hall Press, 1987, pp. 201–28.

Michael Malone, "Tough Puppies," in the *Nation*, Vol. 242, No. 9, March 8, 1986, pp. 276–78, 280.

Review of *The Outsiders*, in the *Times Literary Supplement*, October 30, 1970, p. 1258.

Cynthia Rose, "Rebels Redux: The Fiction of S. E. Hinton," in *Monthly Film Bulletin*, Vol. 50, No. 596, September, 1983, pp. 238–39.

John S. Simmons, "A Look Inside A Landmark: *The Outsiders,"* in *Censored Books: Critical Viewpoints*, edited by Nicholas J. Karolides, Lee Burress, and John M. Kean, The Scarecrow Press, Inc., 1993.

For Further Study

David Ansen, "Coppola Courts the Kiddies," *Newsweek* April 4, 1983, p. 74.

> A review, mostly negative in tone, of Francis Ford Coppola's film version of *The Outsiders.*

Children's Literature Review, Volume 23, Gale, 1991, pp. 132–50.

> A collection of interviews, articles, and reviews on Hinton and her works.

Nicholas Emler and Stephen Reicher, *Adolescence and Delinquency: The Collective Management of Reputation*, Blackwell, 1995.

> After examining the theoretical perspectives on juvenile delinquency by sociology and psychology and dismissing them as based on nineteenth-century thinking, Emler and Reicher ask questions about the context of delinquent behavior in terms of social dynamics. Their questioning leads them to an analysis of identity construction as pursuit or avoidance of delinquent behavior. Finally, they offer solutions through a notion of "reputation management."

Stephen Farber, "Directors Join the S. E. Hinton Fan Club," *New York Times*, March 20, 1983, Section 2, Page 19, Column 2.

> An article which tries to account for the sudden ap-peal of Hinton's books as sources for movie ideas, including quotes from Francis Ford Coppola and Hinton herself.

Randall K. Mills, "The Novels of S. E. Hinton: Springboard to Personal Growth for Adolescents," in *Adolescence*, Vol. XXII, No. 87, Fall, 1987, pp. 641–46.

> An article which examines how teachers may use Hinton's novels to help students explore issues of personal growth.

Wayne S. Wooden, *Renegade Kids, Suburban Outlaws: From Youth Culture to Delinquency (The Wadsworth Contemporary Issues in Crime and Justice)*, Wadsworth Publishing/ITP, 1994.

> Wooden's book is full of qualitative research into youth culture and teen social groups of suburban Los Angeles and it is very accessible to students interested in sociology. He investigates everything from "mall rats" to violent "gangbangers" and skinheads to try to understand what makes "good kids" turn "renegade."